MATHS - E - MASALA

BRATESH KUMAR SINGH

The Dedication for Completing this book goes to Notion Press , Mr. Chauhan Amit Sir , Mr. Brajesh Kumar Sharma Sir , Mr. Mahesh Kumar , Mrs. Sarvesh Kumari , Ms. Brajesh Singh , Mr. Ram Ji Lal ,Mr. Suresh Kumar Singh , Mr. Yuvraj Singh , Mr. Abhimanyu Singh , Mr. Himank Varshney , Mr. Manav Maheshwari .

Contents

Foreword

This Book is being Writen by Mr. BRATESH KUMAR SINGH . I wrote this book because we had seen many Childrens fearing from Maths . Hence , I decided to publish this Book . This is the Part - 1 of this book if you gave good response so we will also be motivated to publish the Part 2 of this Book . We had Inroduced Basic Important Chapters of MATHS .
   - Thanku
   - Author

Preface

Hellow , I am Mr. Bratesh Kumar Singh the writer of this book . I want give a Special Thanks for my Motivational Teachers and all my Team Members . I am very excited to write this book . I wrote this book like this that you can understand this very easily in very simple Language . We also tried to explain it by giving some examples and 1 - 2 Exercises . That makes your practise 100 % .

If you like our book please give feedback to brateshkumarsingh@gmail.com . Your Feedback is very Important to us .

- THANKU
- AUTHOR
- MR. BRATESH KUMAR SINGH

Acknowledgements

Author :- Mr. Bratesh Kumar Singh

Our Motivation :- Mr. Brajesh Kumar Sharma Sir and Mr. Amit Singh Chauhan Sir

Editor - Mr. Bratesh Kumar Singh

Our Team Members - Mr. Mahesh Kumar , Mr. Sarvesh Kumari , Mr. Himank Varshney , Mr. Abhimanyu Singh , Mr. Gaurav Sharma , Mr. Puneet Kumar , Mr. Manav Maheshwari

CHAPTER ONE

Linear Equation in One Variable

;;;A Linear Equation in One Variable means a Equation containing a variable with the highest power 1 . A Linear Equation in One Variable plays an important role in our lives . It allows our idea to be expressed on paper .

It is an equation which is expressed in the form of ax+b = 0, where a and b are two integers, and x is a variable and has only one solution .

For example, 2x+3=8 is a linear equation having a single variable in it .

Here , are five (5) examples with solution .

1) $8x = 40$

Solution: $x = 40/8$

$x = 05$

2) $6x + 5 = 53$

Solution:

$6x = 53 - 5$

$6x = 48$

$x = 48/6$

$x = 8$

3) The sum of 2 numbers is 9 . If we interchange its digit it will be 27 more than the Orignal Number . Find the Number .

Solution: Let , the Ten's Number be = x

So , once no. = 9-x

Orignal Number = (10*x)+9-x

= 10x+9-x

= 9x + 9

Inverted Number = {10*(9-x)} + x

= 90-10x+x

$= 90 - 9x$

A.T.Q

$9x + 9 + 27 = 90 - 9x$

$= 9x + 9x = 90 - 27 - 9$

$= 18x = 54$

$= x = 54/18$

$x = 3$

So , Orignal No. = 36 and Inverted No. = 63 .

4) $(x - 2) + (x - 3) + (x - 9) = 0$

Solution: $(x - 2) + (x - 3) + (x - 9) = 0$

$x - 2 + x - 3 + x - 9 = 0$

$3x - 2 - 3 - 9 = 0$

$3x - 14 = 0$

$x = 14/3$

5) $x/3 - x/2 = 6$

Solution : $x/3 - x/2 = 6$

$x/3 - x/2 = 6$

$(2x - 3x)/6 = 6$

$-x/6 = 6$

$-x = 36$

$x = -36$

Exercise - 1

1 - What is the value of x, of the expressions $3x - 4$?

2 - Which of the following is a linear expression?

(a) x2 +1 (b) y + y2

(c) 4 (d) 1 + z3

3 - The solution of the equation $ax + b = 0$ is ?

4 - The number of boys and girls in a class are in the ratio 5 : 4. If the number of boys is 9 more than the number of girls, then find the number of boys .

5 - The sum of 2 numbers is 11 . If we interchange its digit it will be 9 more than the Orignal Number . Find the Number .

6 - The sum of 2 numbers is 4 . If we interchange its digit it will be (-18) more than the Orignal Number . Find the Number .

7 - The sum of 2 numbers is 9 . If we interchange its digit it will be 9 more than the Orignal Number . Find the Number .

8 - Solve this :- 4x-18=2

9 - Solve this :- 4x + 7 = x + 2

10 - Solve this :- 5x-8 = x +4

CHAPTER TWO

Mensuration - I

In this book Meansuration - I means Area , Perimeter and volume of figures like square , rectrangle and triangle .

Area is the space occupied by an object of a 2- D Figure .

Perimeter is the lenght of an object surronded by the figure .

Volume is the amoung which can be stored in a 3-D figure .

<u>SQUARE</u>

Square is a figure with all sizes equal and having all the angles of 90 degree each .

Area of Square is Side sq . means the space occupied by the square of side x cm.

eg. - Find the area of sq. whose side is 6 cm.

Solution :- Area of Square = side * side

= 6*6

=36 cm.

Perimeter of Square is the sum of all sides as we know perimeter is the length surrounded by an object ; the side of an object surround its object .

Hence , Perimeter of Square = Sum of all sides = 4*Side

eg. Find the perimeter of sq. of side 8 cm.

Solution :- Perimeter of Square = Sum of all sides = 4*Side

= 8*4

= 32

Volume of Cube is the all overall space occupied .

Volume of Cube = a*a*a

eg. Find the volume of a cube whose side is 10

Solution :- Volume of cube = a*a*a

= 10*10*10

= 1000 cm cube

RECTRANGLE

Rectrangle is a figure with opposite side equal and having all the angles of 90 degree each .

Area of Rectrangle is $l * b$ means the space occupied by the Rectrangle of lengh l cm. and breadth b cm.

eg. - Find the area of Rectrangle whose length is 6 cm. and breadth is 5 cm.

Solution :- Area of Rectrangle = l * b

= 6 * 5

= 30 cm.

Perimeter of Rectrangle is the sum of all sides as we know perimeter is the length surrounded by an object ; the side of an object surround its object

.

Hence , Perimeter of Rectrangle = Sum of all sides = l+l+b+b = 2(l+b)

eg. Find the perimeter of Rectrangle of length 9 cm. and breadth 4 cm.

Solution :- Perimeter of Rectrangle = Sum of all sides = 9+9+4+4

= 26 cm.

Volume of Cuboid is the all overall space occupied .

Volume of Cube = l*b*h

eg. Find the volume of a cuboid whose length is 10 , breadth is 5 and height is 15 cm.

Solution :- Volume of cube = l*b*h

= 10*5*15

= 750 cm cube

TRIANGLE

Area of Triangle is $(bh)/2$ means the space occupied by the Triangle of base b cm. and height h cm. divided by 2 i.e half .

eg. - Find the area of Triangle whose base is 8cm. and height $is\ 4$ cm.

Solution :- Area of Triangle = (bh)/2

= (8*4)/2

= 32/2

= 16 cm.

Perimeter of Triangle is the sum of all sides as we know perimeter is the length surrounded by an object ; the side of an object surround its object .
Hence , Perimeter of Triangle = Sum of all sides = a+b+c
eg. Find the perimeter of Triangle of length 9 , 5 and 7 cm.
Solution :- Perimeter of Triangle = Sum of all sides = 9+5+7
= 21 cm.

CHAPTER THREE

Mensuration - II

In this book Meansuration - I means Area , Perimeter of figures Rhombus and Parallelogram .

Rhombus

Rhombus is a figure with all sides equal and its diognal bisect each other at 90 degree .

Area of Rhombus is (diognal1 * diognal2)/2 means the space occupied by the square of Diognal 1 & 2 x and y.

eg. - Find the area of Rhombus whose Diognal are 5 & 9 cm.

Solution :- Area of Rhombus = (d1*d2)/2

= (5*9)/2

=45/2

=22.5 cm.

Perimeter of Rhombus is the sum of all sides as we know perimeter is the length surrounded by an object ; the side of an object surround its object .

Hence , Perimeter of Rhombus = Sum of all sides = 4*a

eg. Find the perimeter of Rhombus of length of side 3 cm.

Solution :- Perimeter of Rhombus = Sum of all sides = 4*3

= 12 cm.

PARALLELOGRAM

Parallelogram is a figure with all opposite equal .

Area of Parallelogram is base * height means the space occupied by the Parallelogram .

eg. - Find the area of Parallelogram whose base and height is 8 & 8 cm.

Solution :- Area of Rhombus = b*h

= 8*8

=64 cm. sq.

Perimeter of Parallelogram is the sum of all sides as we know perimeter is the length surrounded by an object ; the side of an object surround its object .

Hence , Perimeter of Parallelogram = Sum of all sides = 2(a+b)

eg. Find the perimeter of Parallelogram of length 3 cm. and breadth 6 cm.

Solution :- Perimeter of Parallelogram = Sum of all sides = 2(6+3)

= 9*2

= 18 cm. sq.

EXERCISE - 1

Question 1

There are two cuboidal whose dimensions are given below. Which box requires the higher amount of material to make?

Cuboid A: L=23, B=30, H=40

Cuboid B: L=30, B=12, H=44

Question 2

Three cubes, each of edge 2 cm. long are placed together. Find the total surface area of the cuboid so formed?

Question 3

Find the side of a cube whose surface area is 2400 cm2.

Surface of cube= 6a2

So , 6a2=2400

a=20 cm

Question 4

Meghna painted the outside of the cabinet of measure 2 m × 3 m × 2.5 m. How much surface area did she cover if she painted all except the bottom of the cabinet and back side?

Question 5

Ahmed is painting the walls and ceiling of a cuboidal hall with length, breadth and height of 25 m, 12 m and 8 m respectively. From each can of paint 200 m² of area is painted. How many cans of paint will she need to paint the room?

Question 6

A open cylindrical tank of radius 14 m and height 3 m is made from a sheet of metal. How much sheet of metal is required?

Question 7

The lateral surface area of a hollow cylinder is 4224 cm2. It is cut along its height and formed a rectangular sheet of width 33 cm. Find the perimeter of rectangular sheet?

Question 8

A road roller takes 750 complete revolutions to move once over to level a road. Find the area of the road if the diameter of a road roller is 84 cm and length is 1 m.

Question 9

A rectangular sheet of metal foil is 88 cm. long and 20 cm. wide. A cylinder is made out of it, by rolling the foil along width. Find the volume of the cylinder.

Question 10

The perimeter of the floor of a hall is 250 m. If the height is 4 m, find the cost of painting the four walls at the rate of Rs. 12 per square meter.

CHAPTER FOUR

Interest

Interest is amount which we gave when we had taken a borrow or loan from bank or another parties . 0

Interest is of 2 types :- Simple and Compound .

Introduction :-

Interest - Extra money we give when we had taken a loan .

Principle - Total Money we had Borrowed ,

Time - Total period of which we had borrowed money .

Rate - At what rate you will pay interest .

Amount - Total Money you will give after borrowing moneyb . (Principle + Interest)

Profit - Amount more than the C.P

Loss - Amount Less than C.P

Cost Price - Amount in which a product is buyied ,

Sell Price - Amount in which a product selled .

Profit % - Profit in Percentage .

Loss % - Loss in Percentage .

Simple Interest

Simple Interest is the interest which you can find easily . It you know the Principle , Time and Rate .

eg. - Find the interest if P = 25000 , T= 1 year , R = 5%

S.I = (PTR)/100

(25000*1*5)/100

125000/100

1250 = INTEREST

Compound Interest

Compound Interest is the interest which increses year by year . Compound Interest is Amount - Principle .

Amount $= P(1 + R/100)^n$

P = Total money Borrowed , N - No. of years (time)

eg. - Find a Compound Interest of P = 12000 , N- 3 years , R = 5% .

A = 12000(1 + 5/100)^3

12000*21/10*21/10*21/10

13891.5

So, Amount = 13891.5

and C.I = 13891.5 - 12000

= 1891.5

FORMULAS

S.I = (PTR)/100

A = P + I

C.I = A - P

Profit % = Profit / C.P *100

Loss % = Loss / C.P *100

Profit = S.P - C.P

Loss = C,P - S.P

EXERCISE

1) A sum of money at simple interest amounts to Rs. 850 in 3 years and to Rs. 900 in 4years. The sum is:

2) Maninder invested into two different schemes, P and Q at simple interest rate,an amount of Rs. 15,000. Rate of interest for scheme P & Q were 14% p.a. and 18% p.a. respectively. If the total amount of simple interest earned in 2 years be Rs. 5000, what was the amount invested in Scheme P?

3) A sum of Rs. 15,000 amounts to Rs. 19,500 in 5 years at the rate of simple interest. Whatis the rate of interest?

4) How much time will it take for an amount of Rs. 900to yield Rs. 81 as interest at 2.25%per annum of simple interest?

5) A money-lender claims he lends money at simple rate of interest of 10% per annum. But he cleverly tricks the farmers by including the interest amount in the principal when he calculates it every six months. The effective annual rate of interest he is charging is:

6) A sum of money triples itself in 12 years at simple interest. Find the rate of interest?

7) The price of a T.V. set is worth Rs. 20,000 that needs to be paid in 20 installments of Rs. 1,000 each. If the rate of interest be 6% per annum, and the 1st installment be paid at the time of purchase, then the value of the last installment covering the interest will be?

A. Rs. 17,000

8) How much Simple Interest can a person get on Rs. 8,200 at 17.5% p.a. for a period of 2 years and 6 months?

9) In what time will Rs. 4,000 lent at 3% per annum on simple interest earn as much interest as Rs. 5,000 will earn in 5 years at 4% per annum on simple interest?

10) The S.I. on a certain sum of money for 3 years at 8% per annum is half the C.I. on Rs. 4000 for 2 years at 10% per annum. The sum placed on S.I. is?